Knowing the Notes

for cello

by Cassia Harvey

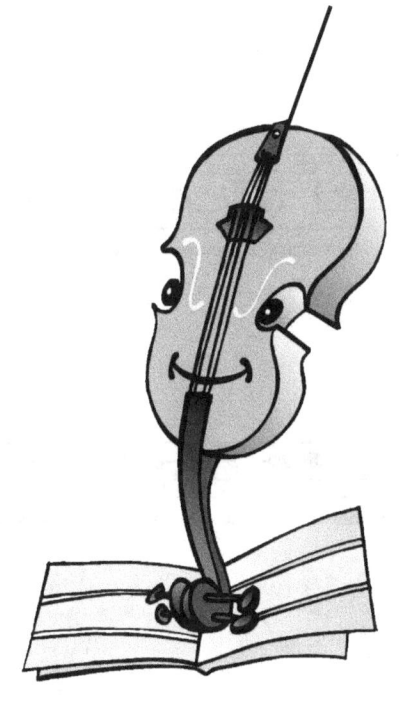

CHP134

©2005 by C. Harvey Publications All Rights Reserved.

www.charveypublications.com - print books
www.learnstrings.com - PDF downloadable books
www.harveystringarrangements.com - chamber music

Knowing the Notes for Cello

The Note D; open string

Cassia Harvey

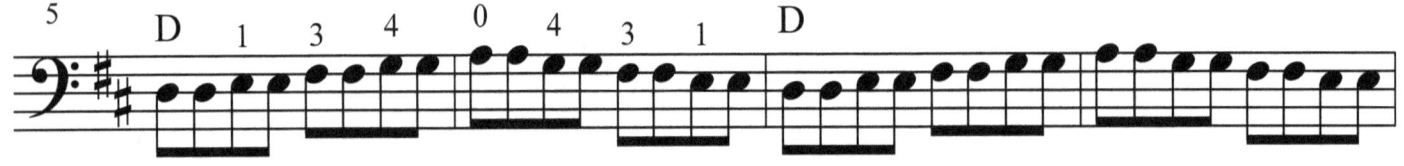

©2005 C. Harvey Publications All Rights Reserved.

Yankee Doodle

Traditional/arr. C. Harvey

How many D notes are in this song?

©2005 C. Harvey Publications All Rights Reserved.

The Note E

The New World and Variation

How many E notes are in this song?

Dvorak/arr. C. Harvey

How many beats are in a measure?

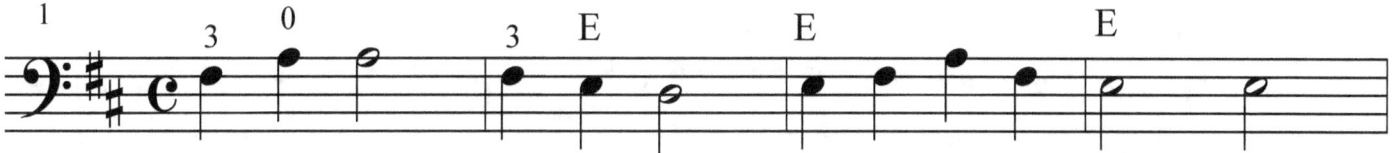

The Note F#

Dance with Variation

How many F# notes are in this song?

Praetorious/arr. C. Harvey

The Note G

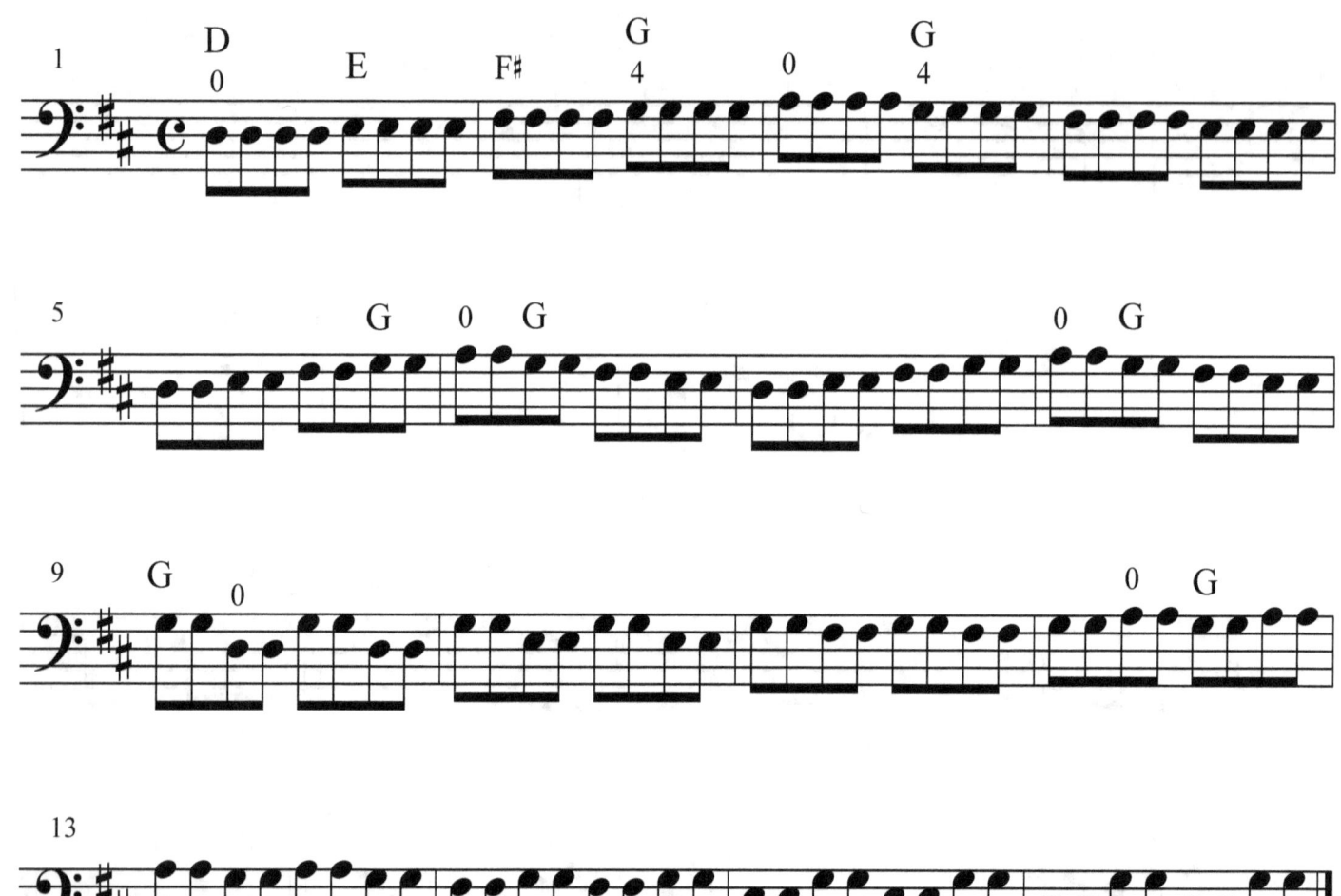

French Dance

How many G notes are in this song?

Traditional/arr. C. Harvey

The Note A; open string

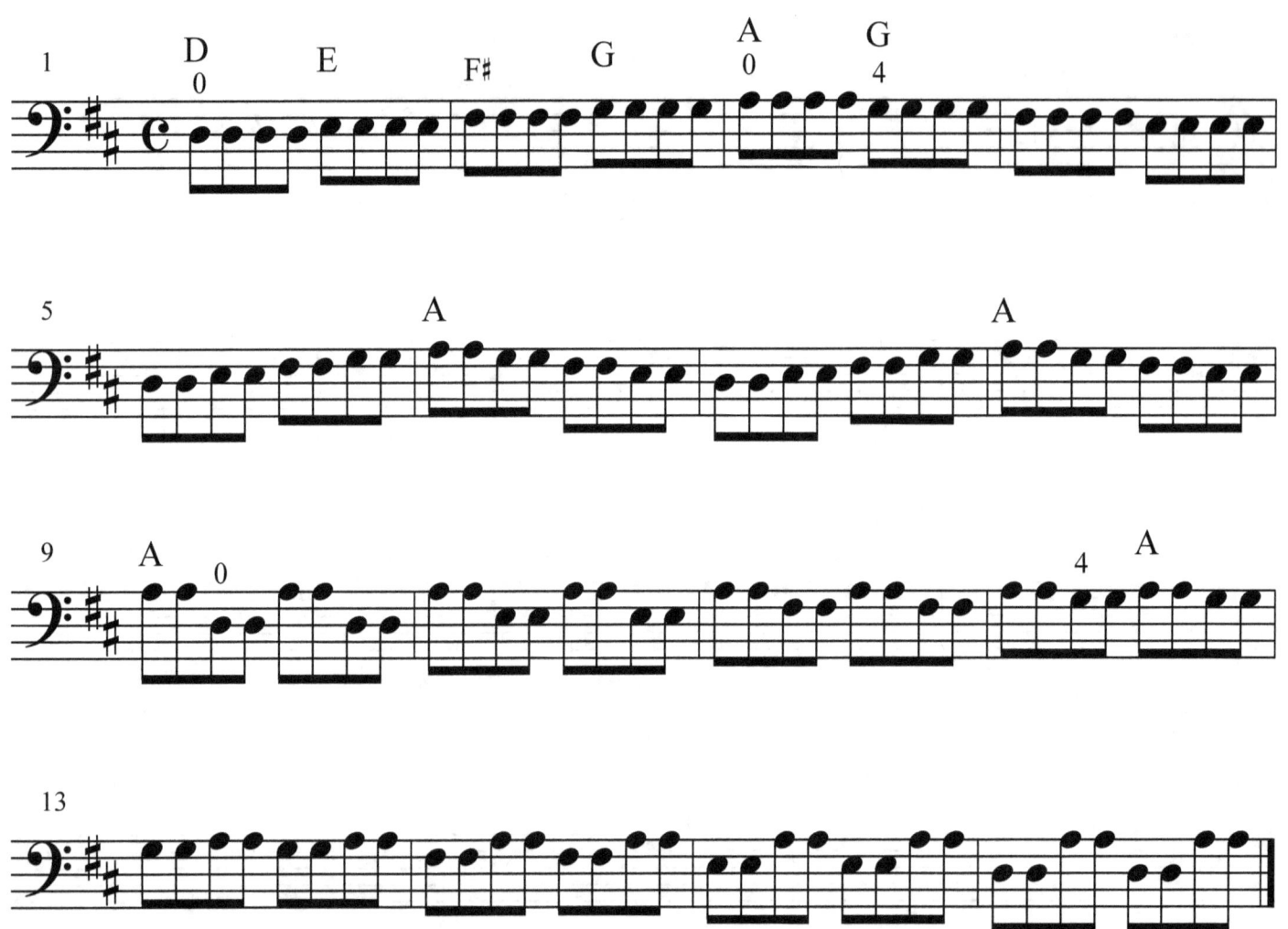

Allegretto

Knowing the Notes for Cello

How many A notes are in this song?

How many beats are in a measure?

Campagnoli/arr. C. Harvey

The Note F♮

Farandole

Bizet/arr. C. Harvey

How many F notes are in this song?

The Note B

Lavender's Blue

Traditional/arr. C. Harvey

The Note C♯

Soldier, Will You Marry Me?

Traditional/arr. C. Harvey

The Note D

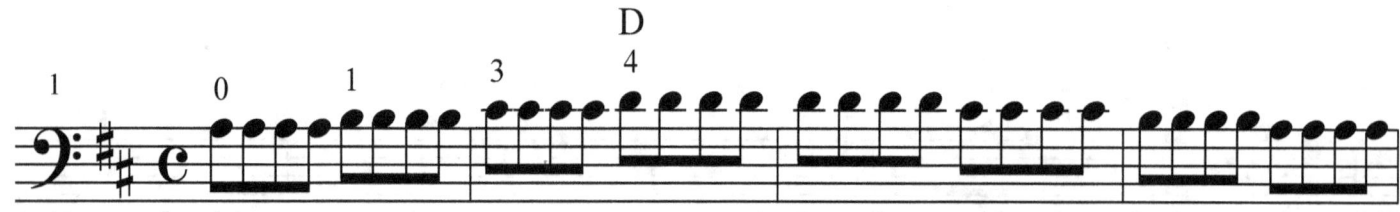

Aiken Drum

Traditional/arr. C. Harvey

The Note C♯

The Prince of Denmark's March

Clarke/arr. C. Harvey

The Note A on the G string

Knowing the Notes for Cello

Cassia Harvey

Drill, Ye Tarriers, Drill

Traditional/arr. C. Harvey

©2005 C. Harvey Publications All Rights Reserved.

The Note B on the G string

Knowing the Notes for Cello

Cassia Harvey

Goober Peas

Traditional/arr. C. Harvey

©2005 C. Harvey Publications All Rights Reserved.

The Note B♭ on the G string

Cassia Harvey

Devil's Dream

Traditional/arr. C. Harvey

©2005 C. Harvey Publications All Rights Reserved.

The Note C; open string

Cassia Harvey

Rigaudon

Rameau/arr. C. Harvey

28

The Note D on the C string
Cassia Harvey

The China Figurine
Rebikov/arr. C. Harvey

©2005 C. Harvey Publications All Rights Reserved.

Knowing the Notes for Cello

The Note E on the C string

Cassia Harvey

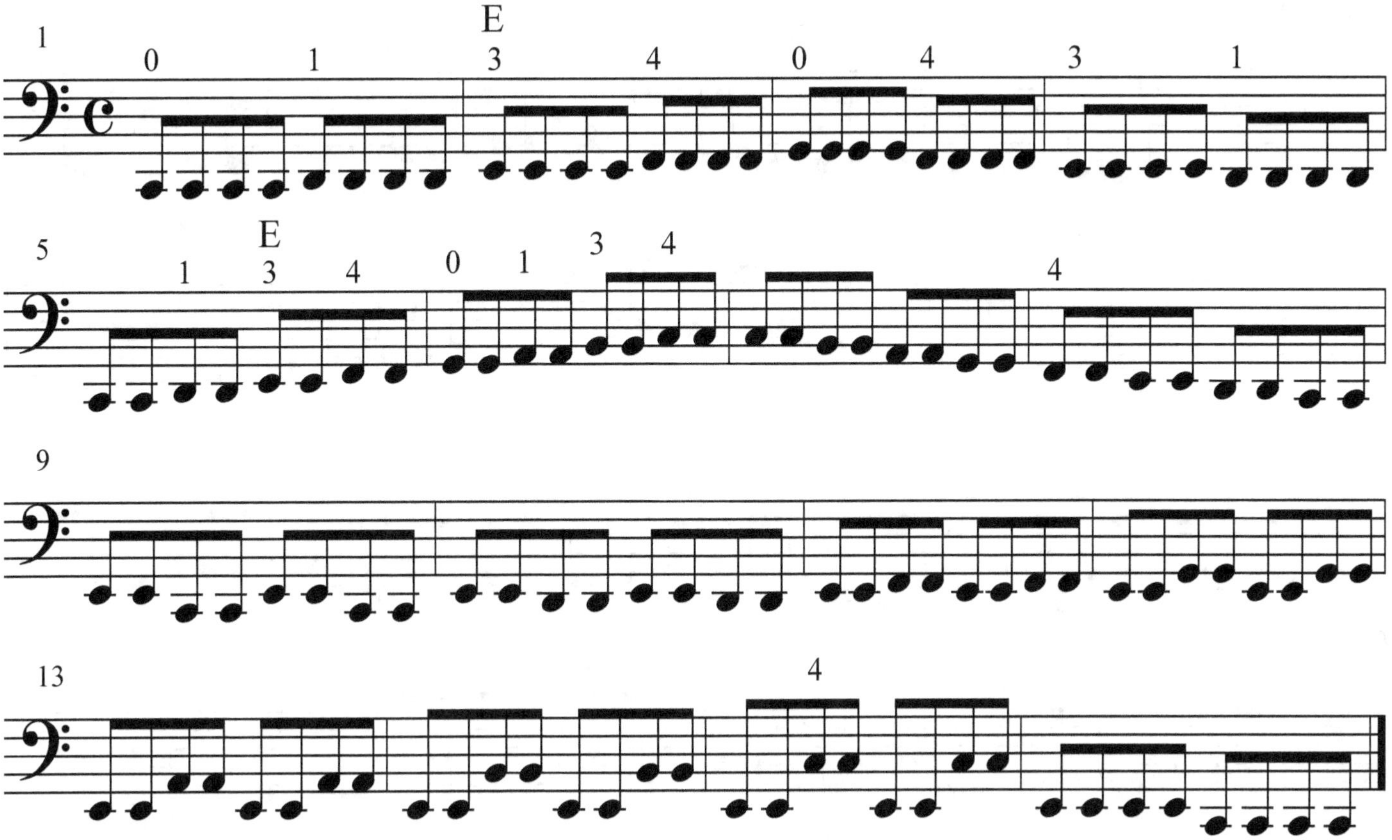

Michael Rowed the Boat Ashore

Traditional/arr. C. Harvey

©2005 C. Harvey Publications All Rights Reserved.

The Note F on the C string

Knowing the Notes for Cello
Cassia Harvey

Allegro

Rameau/arr. C. Harvey

available from www.charveypublications.com: CHP221

Cello Book One

A, B, and C♯

Cassia Harvey

The Ladybug: A Hungarian Folk Song

©2012 C. Harvey Publications All Rights Reserved.

www.ingramcontent.com/pod-product-compliance
Lightning Source LLC
Chambersburg PA
CBHW051428070526
44584CB00023B/3638